American Chronicles

American history, Volume 1

Michael Johnson

Published by Harmony House Publishing, 2024.

While every precaution has been taken in the preparation of this book, the publisher assumes no responsibility for errors or omissions, or for damages resulting from the use of the information contained herein.

AMERICAN CHRONICLES

First edition. March 22, 2024.

Copyright © 2024 Michael Johnson.

ISBN: 979-8224670772

Written by Michael Johnson.

Table of Contents

"To all those who have dared to dream, to strive, and to shape the course of history, this book is dedicated. May the stories within these pages serve as a testament to the resilience, ingenuity, and enduring spirit of the American people. From the indigenous civilizations who first walked this land to the pioneers of progress who continue to push the boundaries of possibility, may we honor their legacy by embracing the lessons of our past as we chart the course for a brighter future. This book is dedicated to the relentless pursuit of truth, justice, and the American dream."

Chapter 1: The Indigenous Peoples

Before the arrival of European explorers and settlers, North America was home to a rich tapestry of indigenous civilizations. These diverse societies had developed over thousands of years, adapting to the varied landscapes and climates of the continent. In this chapter, we will explore the origins, cultures, and societies of these indigenous peoples, as well as the profound impact that European exploration and colonization had on their way of life.

Origins of Indigenous Peoples

The history of indigenous peoples in North America stretches back over millennia, with evidence of human habitation dating back as far as 15,000 years ago. These early inhabitants were hunter-gatherers who migrated across the Bering Land Bridge from Asia into what is now Alaska. Over time, they spread out across the continent, developing distinct cultures and societies.

Diverse Civilizations

The indigenous peoples of North America were incredibly diverse, with hundreds of distinct cultures and languages. In the Arctic region, Inuit and Aleut peoples adapted to the harsh conditions, relying on hunting and fishing for sustenance. Along the Northwest Coast, societies such as the Haida, Tlingit, and Chinook developed complex social structures and thriving economies based on fishing, trade, and artistic expression.

In the Southwest, civilizations such as the Ancestral Puebloans (formerly known as the Anasazi), Hopi, and Navajo built intricate adobe dwellings and mastered techniques such as irrigation farming. The Plains Indians, including the Sioux, Cheyenne, and Blackfoot, were nomadic hunter-gatherers who followed the migratory patterns of bison herds and developed a rich oral tradition.

In the Eastern Woodlands, the Iroquois Confederacy, composed of nations such as the Mohawk, Oneida, and Seneca, established a powerful alliance based on democratic principles and mutual defense. Further south, the Mississippian culture flourished, building elaborate mound complexes such as Cahokia near present-day St. Louis, Missouri.

Impact of European Exploration and Colonization

The arrival of European explorers and settlers in the late 15th and early 16th centuries had a profound impact on the indigenous peoples of North America. Initially, interactions between Europeans and indigenous peoples were characterized by curiosity, trade, and sometimes conflict. However, as European colonization expanded, so too did the displacement, exploitation, and violence against indigenous populations.

Disease and Demographic Collapse

One of the most devastating consequences of European contact was the introduction of infectious diseases such as smallpox, measles, and influenza. These diseases, to which indigenous peoples had no immunity, spread rapidly through native communities, causing widespread death and demographic collapse. Estimates suggest that as much as 90% of the indigenous population may have perished due to disease in the centuries following European contact.

Land Displacement and Treaty Violations

As European settlers expanded their colonies, they forcibly displaced indigenous peoples from their traditional lands, often through violence and coercion. Treaties negotiated between indigenous nations and colonial authorities were frequently ignored or violated, leading to further loss of territory and sovereignty. The process of land dispossession and reservation confinement had profound social, cultural, and economic consequences for indigenous communities.

Cultural Assimilation and Genocide

European colonizers also sought to assimilate indigenous peoples into Eurocentric cultural norms and institutions. Native languages, religions, and cultural practices were suppressed, and children were often forcibly removed from their families and sent to boarding schools designed to eradicate indigenous identity. The deliberate destruction of indigenous cultures and the systematic erasure of indigenous knowledge amounted to a form of cultural genocide.

Resistance and Resilience

Despite the immense challenges they faced, indigenous peoples resisted European colonization through various means, including armed resistance, diplomatic negotiation, and cultural preservation. Leaders such as Tecumseh, Sitting Bull, and Geronimo emerged as symbols of indigenous resistance, challenging colonial expansion and advocating for the rights and sovereignty of their people. Today, indigenous communities continue to assert their rights and cultural heritage, striving to overcome the legacy of colonization and build a future rooted in resilience and self-determination.

Conclusion

The history of the indigenous peoples of North America is one of resilience, adaptation, and survival in the face of profound challenges. From the rich civilizations of the pre-Columbian era to the ongoing struggles for recognition and justice in the modern world, indigenous peoples have played a vital role in shaping the history and identity of the United States. Understanding and honoring their contributions is essential to building a more inclusive and equitable society for all.

Chapter 2: Colonial America

The colonial period in North America marked a pivotal era in the continent's history, as European powers vied for control of new territories and established settlements that would shape the future of the United States. In this chapter, we will explore the motivations behind European exploration and colonization, the establishment of the thirteen colonies, and the social, economic, and political structures that emerged in colonial America.

Exploration and Settlement

Motivations for Exploration

European exploration of the New World was driven by a variety of economic, religious, and political factors. The desire for wealth and resources, including precious metals, spices, and new trade routes to Asia, spurred expeditions sponsored by European monarchs and trading companies. Religious motivations, including the spread of Christianity and the desire to convert indigenous peoples, also played a significant role in exploration efforts. Additionally, European powers sought to expand their territories and assert dominance over rival nations in the race for colonial supremacy.

Early Expeditions

The first European explorers to reach North America were the Norse, who established temporary settlements in present-day Newfoundland and Greenland around the 10th century. However, these Norse colonies were short-lived, and it was not until the late 15th century that sustained European exploration of the Americas began in earnest. In 1492, Christopher Columbus, sponsored by the Spanish crown, made his historic voyage across the Atlantic Ocean, landing in the Caribbean and mistakenly believing he had reached Asia.

Spanish and Portuguese Colonization

Following Columbus's voyages, Spanish and Portuguese explorers embarked on expeditions to claim and colonize the lands they encountered. Spanish conquistadors, such as Hernán Cortés and Francisco Pizarro, conquered vast empires in Central and South America, including the Aztec and Inca civilizations. Portuguese explorers, led by Vasco da Gama and Pedro Álvares Cabral, established trading outposts and colonies along the coast of present-day Brazil.

English Colonization

In the early 17th century, English explorers began to establish permanent settlements in North America, seeking to emulate the success of Spanish and Portuguese colonies. In 1607, the Virginia Company founded Jamestown, the first permanent English settlement in North America, in present-day Virginia. This was followed by the establishment of Plymouth Colony by the Pilgrims in 1620 and the founding of Massachusetts Bay Colony by the Puritans in 1630.

Dutch and French Colonization

In addition to the English, other European powers established colonies in North America during the colonial period. The Dutch established New Netherland, centered on present-day New York City, as a trading outpost in the early 17th century. The French, meanwhile, established a network of fur trading posts and settlements in the Great Lakes region and along the Mississippi River, including Quebec and New Orleans.

Establishment of the Thirteen Colonies

New England Colonies

The New England colonies, including Massachusetts, Connecticut, Rhode Island, and New Hampshire, were characterized by their Puritan religious beliefs, small-scale farming, and maritime economy. These colonies were founded by religious dissenters seeking religious freedom and economic opportunity in the New World. Town meetings and a strong sense of community were central to the social and political life of New England.

Middle Colonies

The middle colonies, including New York, New Jersey, Pennsylvania, and Delaware, were known for their diverse population, fertile soil, and thriving trade networks. These colonies attracted immigrants from various European countries, including England, the Netherlands, Sweden, and Germany, creating a multicultural society. Agriculture, commerce, and manufacturing were the primary economic activities in the middle colonies.

Southern Colonies

The southern colonies, including Virginia, Maryland, North Carolina, South Carolina, and Georgia, were characterized by large plantations, cash crop agriculture, and a hierarchical society based on race and class. The cultivation of crops such as tobacco, rice, and indigo relied heavily on enslaved labor imported from Africa. The plantation system dominated the economy and social structure of the southern colonies.

Social, Economic, and Political Structures

Social Structure

Colonial society was hierarchical, with wealth, status, and power concentrated in the hands of a small elite of landowners, merchants, and political leaders. Below them were yeoman farmers, artisans, and laborers, followed by enslaved Africans and indigenous peoples, who occupied the lowest rungs of the social ladder. Despite these divisions, colonial society was also characterized by a degree of social mobility and opportunity for those willing to work hard and seize opportunities.

Economic Structure

The colonial economy was diverse and multifaceted, with each region developing its own economic base and specialization. In New England, shipbuilding, fishing, trade, and small-scale farming were important economic activities. The middle colonies developed a thriving agricultural economy based on the cultivation of grains, livestock, and cash crops such as wheat and corn.

In the southern colonies, plantation agriculture, centered on the production of crops like tobacco, rice, and indigo, dominated the economy.

Political Structure

Colonial governments were characterized by a mix of representative and authoritarian elements, with power divided between colonial assemblies, appointed governors, and colonial charters granted by the English monarch. In New England, town meetings and colonial assemblies provided opportunities for political participation and self-governance. In the middle and southern colonies, colonial governments were often dominated by wealthy landowners and merchants who wielded significant influence over political decisions.

Conclusion

The colonial period in North America was a time of exploration, conquest, and settlement, as European powers established colonies that would eventually become the foundation of the United States. The thirteen colonies that emerged during this period were characterized by diverse social, economic, and political structures, shaped by factors such as geography, culture, and religion. Understanding the complexities of colonial America is essential to grasping the origins and development of the United States as a nation.

Chapter 3: The Revolutionary War

The Revolutionary War, also known as the American War of Independence, was a pivotal conflict that marked the birth of the United States as a sovereign nation. In this chapter, we will explore the causes of the American Revolution, the key events and figures that led to independence, and the formation of the United States and the writing of the Constitution.

Causes of the American Revolution

Taxation without Representation

One of the primary grievances that fueled the American Revolution was the issue of taxation without representation. The British government imposed a series of taxes on the American colonies, including the Stamp Act, the Townshend Acts, and the Tea Act, without the consent of the colonists. This violation of the principle of "no taxation without representation" led to widespread protests and resistance in the colonies.

Restrictive Colonial Policies

In addition to taxation, the British government imposed a series of restrictive policies on the American colonies, including the Quartering Act, which required colonists to house and feed British troops, and the Intolerable Acts, which punished the residents of Massachusetts for their role in the Boston Tea Party. These policies were seen as oppressive and unjust by many colonists, further fueling resentment towards British rule.

Economic Grievances

Economic factors also played a significant role in the lead-up to the American Revolution. The British government imposed trade restrictions and regulations that favored British merchants and manufacturers over their American counterparts. Additionally, the colonies faced economic hardship due to currency shortages, inflation, and debt, exacerbated by the costs of maintaining British troops in North America.

Ideals of Liberty and Self-Government

The American Revolution was also driven by a desire for liberty, self-government, and independence from British rule. Influenced by Enlightenment ideas of natural rights, individual freedom, and representative government, American colonists began to assert their rights and challenge the authority of the British monarchy. The writings of thinkers such as John Locke, Thomas Paine, and Thomas Jefferson articulated the principles of liberty and democracy that would inspire the revolutionaries.

Key Events and Figures Leading to Independence

Boston Massacre (1770)

The Boston Massacre, which occurred on March 5, 1770, was a pivotal event that inflamed tensions between the colonists and the British authorities. In response to growing unrest and protests in Boston, British soldiers fired into a crowd of colonists, killing five people. The incident galvanized public opinion against British rule and fueled calls for independence.

Boston Tea Party (1773)

The Boston Tea Party, which took place on December 16, 1773, was a defiant act of protest against British taxation and monopoly control over the tea trade. Disguised as Mohawk Indians, a group of colonists boarded British ships in Boston Harbor and dumped chests of tea into the water in protest of the Tea Act. The event sparked outrage in Britain and led to the passage of the Intolerable Acts.

Battles of Lexington and Concord (1775)

The Battles of Lexington and Concord, fought on April 19, 1775, marked the beginning of armed conflict between British troops and American colonists. British forces were sent to seize colonial munitions stockpiled in Concord, Massachusetts, but were met with resistance from local militia forces at Lexington. The battles served as a rallying cry for American patriots and galvanized support for the revolution.

Declaration of Independence (1776)

On July 4, 1776, the Continental Congress adopted the Declaration of Independence, proclaiming the thirteen American colonies as independent states no longer under British rule. Drafted primarily by Thomas Jefferson, the Declaration articulated the principles of liberty, equality, and self-government that would define the new nation. The signing of the Declaration marked the formal beginning of the American Revolution.

Formation of the United States and the Writing of the Constitution

Articles of Confederation (1777)

Following the Declaration of Independence, the Continental Congress drafted the Articles of Confederation as the first constitution of the United States. Adopted in 1777, the Articles established a weak central government with limited powers, leaving most authority to the individual states. However, the Articles proved ineffective in governing the new nation and addressing its economic and political challenges.

Constitutional Convention (1787)

Recognizing the need for a stronger central government, delegates from the thirteen states convened in Philadelphia in 1787 to draft a new constitution. The Constitutional Convention, chaired by George Washington, included prominent figures such as James Madison, Alexander Hamilton, and Benjamin Franklin. Over the course of several months, the delegates debated and negotiated the structure and powers of the new federal government.

Ratification and Bill of Rights

After much debate and compromise, the Constitution was signed on September 17, 1787, and submitted to the states for ratification. However, ratification was not without controversy, as critics expressed concerns about the concentration of power in the federal government and the lack of protections for individual rights. To address these concerns, the Bill of Rights, consisting of the first ten amendments to the Constitution, was added to guarantee fundamental liberties such as freedom of speech, religion, and due process.

Establishment of the United States

With the ratification of the Constitution in 1788, the United States of America officially came into existence as a federal republic. George Washington was elected as the nation's first president in 1789, and the new government began to function under the framework established by the Constitution. The principles of liberty, democracy, and self-government that inspired the American Revolution were enshrined in the founding documents of the United States, laying the foundation for the nation's future development and prosperity.

Conclusion

The Revolutionary War and the founding of the United States represent a transformative moment in world history, as a group of colonies broke away from the British Empire to form a new nation based on the principles of liberty, equality, and self-government. The causes of the American Revolution, the key events and figures that led to independence, and the formation of the United States and the writing of the Constitution are essential to understanding the origins and ideals of the American republic.

Chapter 4: The Early Republic

The period following the American Revolution marked the dawn of the Early Republic, a time of experimentation, growth, and challenges as the fledgling nation sought to establish its identity and governance. In this chapter, we will explore the challenges faced by the new nation under the Articles of Confederation, the development of political parties and the presidency of George Washington, and the monumental event of the Louisiana Purchase and westward expansion.

Challenges Faced by the New Nation under the Articles of Confederation

Weak Central Government

The Articles of Confederation, adopted in 1781, established a decentralized system of government with a weak central authority. Under the Articles, the national government lacked the power to levy taxes, regulate commerce, or enforce its laws. Instead, most authority resided with the individual states, leading to a lack of cohesion and cooperation among the states and hindering effective governance.

Economic Instability

The lack of centralized economic authority under the Articles of Confederation contributed to economic instability and uncertainty. The national government had no power to regulate trade or currency, leading to disputes over tariffs and trade barriers between states. Additionally, the inability to levy taxes left the government unable to repay its debts from the Revolutionary War, leading to financial difficulties and inflation.

Shays' Rebellion

One of the most significant challenges faced by the new nation under the Articles of Confederation was Shays' Rebellion, a revolt by Massachusetts farmers in 1786-1787. The farmers, burdened by high taxes and debts, rebelled against the state government, seizing courthouses and disrupting the legal system. The rebellion highlighted the weaknesses of the Articles of Confederation and the need for a stronger central government capable of maintaining order and stability.

Development of Political Parties and the Presidency of George Washington

Formation of Political Parties

The development of political parties in the United States can be traced back to the presidency of George Washington and the debate over the role and powers of the federal government. Two main factions emerged during Washington's administration: the Federalists, led by Alexander Hamilton, and the Democratic-Republicans, led by Thomas Jefferson. The Federalists favored a strong central government and policies that promoted commerce and industry, while the Democratic-Republicans advocated for states' rights and agrarian interests.

Hamilton's Financial Plan

As Secretary of the Treasury under President Washington, Alexander Hamilton developed a series of economic policies aimed at stabilizing the nation's finances and promoting economic growth. Hamilton's plan included the assumption of state debts, the establishment of a national bank, and the imposition of tariffs and excise taxes. While controversial, Hamilton's financial plan laid the foundation for a strong federal government and modern economy.

Washington's Farewell Address

In his Farewell Address to the nation in 1796, George Washington warned against the dangers of political factions and foreign entanglements. He urged Americans to remain united as a nation and to avoid the pitfalls of partisan politics. Washington's Farewell Address is considered a seminal moment in American political history and continues to resonate as a call for national unity and civic virtue.

The Louisiana Purchase and Westward Expansion

Louisiana Purchase (1803)

One of the most significant events of the Early Republic was the Louisiana Purchase, in which the United States acquired over 800,000 square miles of territory from France for $15 million. The purchase, negotiated by President Thomas Jefferson, doubled the size of the United States and opened up vast new opportunities for westward expansion. The acquisition of the Louisiana Territory laid the groundwork for the expansion of American influence and settlement across the continent.

Lewis and Clark Expedition

In 1804, President Jefferson commissioned Meriwether Lewis and William Clark to explore the newly acquired Louisiana Territory and to find a water route to the Pacific Ocean. The Lewis and Clark Expedition, also known as the Corps of Discovery, journeyed westward from St. Louis, Missouri, to the Pacific coast, mapping the terrain, studying the flora and fauna, and establishing diplomatic relations with Native American tribes. The expedition played a crucial role in expanding American knowledge of the continent and paving the way for further westward expansion.

Manifest Destiny

The concept of Manifest Destiny, popularized in the 19th century, embodied the belief that it was the destiny of the United States to expand across the North American continent from the Atlantic to the Pacific. Manifest Destiny fueled westward expansion, spurred by economic opportunities, territorial ambitions, and a sense of national mission. The acquisition of territories such as Oregon, Texas, and California further solidified American control over the continent and shaped the nation's identity and destiny.

Conclusion

The Early Republic was a formative period in American history, marked by challenges, innovation, and expansion. From the struggles of governance under the Articles of Confederation to the development of political parties and the presidency of George Washington, and the monumental events of the Louisiana Purchase and westward expansion, this period laid the groundwork for the growth and development of the United States as a nation. The ideals of liberty, democracy, and opportunity that emerged during this time continue to shape the identity and aspirations of the American people.

Chapter 5: The Age of Jackson

The Age of Jackson, spanning from the late 1820s to the early 1840s, was a transformative period in American history characterized by the presidency of Andrew Jackson, the expansion of democracy and voting rights, and the doctrine of Manifest Destiny. In this chapter, we will delve into the presidency of Andrew Jackson and its impact on American politics, the expansion of democracy and voting rights during this time, and the consequences of Manifest Destiny for the nation.

Andrew Jackson's Presidency and its Impact on American Politics

Rise to Power

Andrew Jackson, a military hero and populist politician, rose to prominence in the early 19th century as a champion of the common man and opponent of entrenched political elites. Born in the frontier region of the Carolinas, Jackson gained fame as a general during the War of 1812, particularly for his victory at the Battle of New Orleans. Jackson's popularity as a military leader propelled him into politics, and he was elected as the seventh president of the United States in 1828.

Jacksonian Democracy

Jackson's presidency ushered in a new era of American politics known as Jacksonian Democracy, characterized by the expansion of suffrage, the rise of political parties, and the growth of populist sentiment. Jackson sought to decentralize power and promote the interests of ordinary citizens over entrenched elites, a philosophy encapsulated in his famous slogan, "The people's president."

Spoils System

One of the most significant changes Jackson implemented was the introduction of the spoils system, in which political supporters were rewarded with government positions and patronage. Jackson's use of the spoils system helped to solidify his political base and strengthen the Democratic Party, but it also led to charges of corruption and cronyism.

Nullification Crisis

A defining moment of Jackson's presidency was the Nullification Crisis, a constitutional showdown between the federal government and the state of South Carolina over tariffs. In response to the Tariff of Abominations, which imposed high tariffs on imported goods, South Carolina declared the tariff null and void within its borders and threatened to secede from the Union. Jackson, a staunch defender of federal authority, issued a proclamation condemning nullification and threatened to use military force to enforce federal law. The crisis was ultimately resolved through a compromise tariff negotiated by Henry Clay.

Indian Removal

Another controversial aspect of Jackson's presidency was his policy of Indian removal, which sought to relocate Native American tribes from their ancestral lands in the southeastern United States to territories west of the Mississippi River. The Indian Removal Act of 1830 authorized the federal government to negotiate treaties with Native American tribes for their removal to the west, leading to the forced relocation of tens of thousands of Native Americans along the Trail of Tears.

Expansion of Democracy and Voting Rights

Universal White Male Suffrage

The Age of Jackson witnessed the expansion of democracy and voting rights in the United States, as states abolished property ownership requirements and other restrictions on suffrage, leading to the widespread adoption of universal white male suffrage. The elimination of property qualifications allowed a broader segment of the population to participate in the political process and helped to democratize American society.

Rise of Political Parties

The Age of Jackson also saw the rise of political parties as powerful forces in American politics. Jackson's Democratic Party, formed in the 1820s, emerged as the dominant political force in the country, advocating for states' rights, limited government, and the expansion of democracy. The opposition Whig Party, founded in the 1830s, represented a coalition of anti-Jackson forces, including former National Republicans, states' rights advocates, and supporters of protective tariffs and internal improvements.

Expansion of Suffrage for Women and Free African Americans

While the expansion of democracy during the Age of Jackson primarily benefited white males, there were also efforts to extend suffrage to other groups. In some states, women and free African Americans gained the right to vote in local and state elections, although these gains were often short-lived and limited in scope. Nevertheless, the push for universal suffrage laid the groundwork for future movements for women's rights and civil rights.

Manifest Destiny and its Consequences

Expansionist Ideology

Manifest Destiny was the belief that it was America's destiny and duty to expand its territory across the North American continent, from the Atlantic to the Pacific. This expansionist ideology was fueled by a combination of territorial ambition, economic opportunity, and a sense of national mission.

Westward Expansion

The doctrine of Manifest Destiny drove westward expansion across the continent, as pioneers, settlers, and entrepreneurs sought to claim new lands and resources. The acquisition of territories such as Texas, Oregon, and California through treaties, purchase, and conquest furthered America's territorial ambitions and transformed the nation into a transcontinental power.

Conflict with Native Americans

Westward expansion also led to conflict with Native American tribes who resisted encroachment on their lands and way of life. The Indian Wars, fought throughout the 19th century, were marked by violence, displacement, and the loss of Native American territory and sovereignty. The policy of Indian removal, pursued by Jackson and subsequent administrations, resulted in the forced relocation of thousands of Native Americans and the loss of countless lives.

Territorial Disputes and International Relations

The doctrine of Manifest Destiny also had consequences for America's relations with other nations, particularly Mexico and Britain. The annexation of Texas and the Oregon Territory, as well as the Mexican-American War, fueled tensions with Mexico and eventually led to the acquisition of vast territories in the Southwest and West. Similarly, territorial disputes with Britain over the Oregon border and the ownership of the Pacific Northwest were resolved through diplomacy and negotiation.

Conclusion

The Age of Jackson was a period of profound change and transformation in American history, characterized by the presidency of Andrew Jackson, the expansion of democracy and voting rights, and the doctrine of Manifest Destiny. Jackson's presidency ushered in a new era of American politics marked by populism, party politics, and the expansion of suffrage. The expansionist ideology of Manifest Destiny drove westward expansion across the continent, leading to conflict, conquest, and the remaking of the American landscape. The legacy of the Age of Jackson continues to shape American politics, society, and identity to this day, as the nation grapples with questions of democracy, equality, and justice.

Chapter 6: Antebellum America

The antebellum period in America, spanning from the early 19th century to the outbreak of the Civil War in 1861, was marked by profound social, economic, and political changes that laid the groundwork for the conflict over slavery and the nation's eventual division. In this chapter, we will explore the social and economic developments in the North and South, the abolitionist movement and the growing divide over slavery, and the Compromise of 1850 and the Kansas-Nebraska Act, which exacerbated tensions leading to the Civil War.

Social and Economic Developments in the North and South

The Northern Economy

In the North, the antebellum period witnessed the rapid growth of industrialization, urbanization, and commercial agriculture. The invention of new technologies, such as the cotton gin and the mechanized loom, revolutionized manufacturing and spurred the rise of textile mills, factories, and urban centers. Cities such as Boston, New York, and Philadelphia became bustling hubs of commerce and industry, attracting immigrants from Europe and rural migrants from the countryside. The Northern economy was characterized by wage labor, free enterprise, and a diverse array of industries, including textiles, shipping, finance, and manufacturing.

The Southern Economy

In contrast, the Southern economy remained primarily agrarian and rural, centered on plantation agriculture, particularly the cultivation of cotton, tobacco, rice, and sugar. The invention of the cotton gin by Eli Whitney in 1793 led to a boom in cotton production and the expansion of slavery in the South. Plantation owners relied on enslaved labor to work their vast estates, leading to the concentration of wealth and power in the hands of a small planter elite. The Southern economy was characterized by the plantation system, a hierarchical social structure based on race and class, and a dependence on agricultural exports for economic prosperity.

Social Hierarchies

The antebellum South was characterized by strict social hierarchies based on race, class, and gender. At the top of the social ladder were wealthy white planters who owned large estates and enslaved labor. Below them were white yeoman farmers, artisans, and laborers, who owned smaller farms or worked as hired hands. Enslaved Africans and African Americans occupied the lowest rungs of the social hierarchy, denied basic rights and subjected to brutal exploitation and violence.

Immigration and Urbanization

In the North, the antebellum period saw a wave of immigration from Europe, particularly Ireland and Germany, driven by economic hardship, political upheaval, and the promise of opportunity in America. Immigrants settled in cities such as New York, Boston, and Philadelphia, where they found work in factories, mills, and construction projects. Urbanization led to the growth of slums, overcrowded tenements, and social problems such as poverty, crime, and disease. Despite these challenges, cities became centers of cultural diversity, social activism, and political mobilization.

The Abolitionist Movement and the Growing Divide over Slavery

Rise of Abolitionism

The antebellum period witnessed the rise of the abolitionist movement, a grassroots campaign to end slavery and promote racial equality in America. Inspired by religious faith, moral conviction, and Enlightenment ideals of liberty and justice, abolitionists such as William Lloyd Garrison, Frederick Douglass, Harriet Tubman, and Sojourner Truth waged a relentless struggle against the institution of slavery. Abolitionists organized lectures, pamphlets, newspapers, and petitions, calling for the immediate emancipation of enslaved Africans and the abolition of slavery in the United States.

Growing Sectional Tensions

The abolitionist movement fueled growing sectional tensions between the North and South over the issue of slavery. Abolitionists denounced slavery as a moral evil and a violation of human rights, while defenders of slavery argued that it was a necessary and benevolent institution that provided for the economic prosperity and social stability of the South. The debate over slavery intensified as the nation expanded westward, leading to conflicts over the extension of slavery into new territories and states.

Fugitive Slave Act

In 1850, Congress passed the Fugitive Slave Act as part of the Compromise of 1850, which required Northern states to assist in the capture and return of escaped slaves to their owners in the South. The Fugitive Slave Act outraged abolitionists and sparked protests and resistance in the North, where sympathy for the plight of enslaved Africans was growing. The act further deepened the divide between North and South and fueled anti-slavery sentiment in the Northern states.

The Compromise of 1850 and the Kansas-Nebraska Act

Compromise of 1850

The Compromise of 1850 was a series of legislative measures designed to address the issue of slavery and the growing sectional divide between North and South. The compromise included provisions such as the admission of California as a free state, the establishment of popular sovereignty in the territories of New Mexico and Utah, and the passage of the Fugitive Slave Act. While the compromise temporarily defused tensions over slavery, it ultimately failed to resolve the underlying conflicts and served to delay the inevitable confrontation over the institution of slavery.

Kansas-Nebraska Act

The Kansas-Nebraska Act of 1854 repealed the Missouri Compromise of 1820 and allowed for the organization of the Kansas and Nebraska territories with popular sovereignty on the question of slavery. The act sparked a bitter conflict between pro-slavery and anti-slavery settlers in Kansas, leading to a series of violent confrontations known as "Bleeding Kansas." The violence in Kansas further inflamed tensions between North and South and hastened the onset of the Civil War.

Conclusion

The antebellum period in America was a time of profound social, economic, and political change, characterized by the rise of industrialization in the North, the expansion of plantation agriculture in the South, the growth of the abolitionist movement, and the deepening divide over the issue of slavery. The Compromise of 1850 and the Kansas-Nebraska Act temporarily mitigated tensions over slavery but ultimately failed to resolve the underlying conflicts between North and South. The stage was set for the outbreak of the Civil War, which would ultimately determine the fate of slavery and the future of the nation.

Chapter 7: The Civil War

The Civil War, fought from 1861 to 1865, was the deadliest conflict in American history, pitting the Northern states of the Union against the Southern states of the Confederacy in a struggle over the future of the nation and the institution of slavery. In this chapter, we will explore the causes of the Civil War, including sectionalism and slavery, the key battles and turning points of the war, and the impact of the war on American society.

Causes of the Civil War

Sectionalism

One of the primary causes of the Civil War was sectionalism, the deepening divide between the Northern and Southern states over political, economic, and social issues. Sectional tensions had been simmering for decades, fueled by differences in culture, economy, and ideology between the North and South. The North, with its burgeoning industrial economy and growing population, advocated for policies that favored free labor, economic development, and federal authority. In contrast, the South, with its agrarian economy based on plantation agriculture and reliance on enslaved labor, defended states' rights, the institution of slavery, and the preservation of its way of life.

Slavery

At the heart of the sectional conflict was the issue of slavery, which had been a divisive issue since the founding of the nation. The expansion of slavery into new territories and states, the fugitive slave laws, and the debates over the status of slavery in the western territories intensified tensions between North and South. While some Northern states had abolished slavery or enacted gradual emancipation laws, the institution remained deeply entrenched in the South, where it was central to the economy, society, and culture.

States' Rights vs. Federal Authority

The question of states' rights versus federal authority was another key issue that contributed to the outbreak of the Civil War. Southern states argued for the principle of states' rights, asserting that individual states had the right to nullify federal laws they deemed unconstitutional or to secede from the Union altogether. Northern states, on the other hand, advocated for a strong federal government with broad powers to regulate commerce, levy taxes, and enforce laws, including those related to slavery.

Political Polarization

The political polarization of the nation in the years leading up to the Civil War further exacerbated tensions between North and South. The emergence of radical abolitionists in the North, such as William Lloyd Garrison and John Brown, who advocated for the immediate emancipation of enslaved Africans and the overthrow of the slave system, alarmed Southerners and hardened their resolve to defend their way of life. Meanwhile, the rise of pro-slavery extremists in the South, who advocated for the expansion of slavery into new territories and states, further inflamed passions and pushed the nation closer to the brink of war.

Key Battles and Turning Points of the War

Fort Sumter (1861)

The Civil War began on April 12, 1861, when Confederate forces bombarded Fort Sumter, a Union garrison located in Charleston Harbor, South Carolina. The attack on Fort Sumter marked the beginning of hostilities between North and South and galvanized public opinion in both regions. President Abraham Lincoln's call for volunteers to suppress the rebellion led to the secession of additional Southern states and the escalation of the conflict into full-scale war.

First Battle of Bull Run (1861)

The first major engagement of the Civil War took place on July 21, 1861, near Manassas, Virginia, at the First Battle of Bull Run (also known as the First Battle of Manassas). The battle was a Confederate victory, as Southern forces under General P.G.T. Beauregard routed Union troops led by General Irvin McDowell. The shocking defeat at Bull Run shattered Northern illusions of a quick and easy victory and underscored the long and bloody struggle that lay ahead.

Battle of Antietam (1862)

The Battle of Antietam, fought on September 17, 1862, near Sharpsburg, Maryland, was the bloodiest single day in American history, with over 23,000 casualties. The battle ended in a tactical draw but was a strategic victory for the Union, as it halted Confederate General Robert E. Lee's invasion of the North and provided President Lincoln with the opportunity to issue the Emancipation Proclamation.

Gettysburg (1863)

The Battle of Gettysburg, fought from July 1 to July 3, 1863, in Gettysburg, Pennsylvania, was the largest and bloodiest battle of the Civil War. The Union victory at Gettysburg, coupled with General Ulysses S. Grant's victory at Vicksburg, Mississippi, which occurred on the same day, marked a turning point in the war. The Confederate defeat at Gettysburg dashed hopes of a Southern invasion of the North and dealt a severe blow to Confederate morale.

Sherman's March to the Sea (1864)

In 1864, Union General William Tecumseh Sherman led a devastating campaign through Georgia known as Sherman's March to the Sea. Sherman's army, numbering over 60,000 men, marched from Atlanta to Savannah, destroying railroads, bridges, and civilian infrastructure along the way. The campaign inflicted widespread destruction and demoralized the Southern population, contributing to the collapse of Confederate resistance.

Appomattox Court House (1865)

The Civil War effectively ended on April 9, 1865, when Confederate General Robert E. Lee surrendered his army to Union General Ulysses S. Grant at Appomattox Court House, Virginia. The surrender at Appomattox signaled the collapse of the Confederate cause and the beginning of the process of Reconstruction, as the nation sought to heal the wounds of war and rebuild a shattered Union.

The Emancipation Proclamation and the Impact of

the War on American Society

Emancipation Proclamation (1863)

One of the most significant events of the Civil War was President Abraham Lincoln's issuance of the Emancipation Proclamation on January 1, 1863. The proclamation declared that all enslaved Africans in Confederate-held territory were to be set free, effectively transforming the war into a struggle for the abolition of slavery. While the Emancipation Proclamation did not immediately free all enslaved Africans, as it exempted border states and areas under Union control, it signaled a fundamental shift in the Union's war aims and helped to galvanize support for the Union cause both at home and abroad.

Impact on American Society

The Civil War had a profound impact on American society, transforming the nation politically, socially, and economically. The war led to the abolition of slavery in the United States, ending one of the most contentious and morally reprehensible institutions in American history. The emancipation of enslaved Africans, followed by the passage of the 13th, 14th, and 15th Amendments to the Constitution, which abolished slavery, granted citizenship and equal protection under the law to all citizens, and guaranteed voting rights regardless of race, marked a significant step toward racial equality and justice in America.

Economic Transformation

The Civil War also brought about profound economic changes, as the war effort spurred industrialization, infrastructure development, and technological innovation. The demands of war production led to the growth of factories, railroads, and manufacturing industries in the North, laying the foundation for America's emergence as an industrial powerhouse in the late 19th and early 20th centuries. In the South, the war devastated the economy and destroyed the institution of slavery, leading to widespread poverty and economic hardship in the aftermath of the war. The destruction of property, loss of labor, and collapse of the plantation system left the Southern economy in ruins, setting the stage for the challenges of Reconstruction.

Social Change and Reconstruction

The Civil War and emancipation also brought about significant social change in American society. The end of slavery fundamentally altered the status and rights of African Americans, who emerged from bondage as free individuals with newfound opportunities and aspirations. However, the promise of freedom was often met with violence, discrimination, and resistance from white supremacists who sought to maintain the racial hierarchy of the antebellum South. The period of Reconstruction, which followed the Civil War, saw efforts to rebuild the South, extend civil rights to freedmen, and reshape the political landscape of the nation.

Legacy of the Civil War

The legacy of the Civil War continues to reverberate in American society to this day, shaping the nation's identity, values, and political landscape. The war remains a potent symbol of the struggle for freedom, equality, and justice, as well as the enduring divisions and challenges that continue to plague the nation. The memory of the Civil War is enshrined in monuments, memorials, and commemorations across the country, reminding Americans of the sacrifices made and the lessons learned from this defining chapter in their history.

Conclusion

The Civil War was a watershed moment in American history, a cataclysmic conflict that tested the nation's ideals, institutions, and unity to their limits. The causes of the war, including sectionalism, slavery, and political polarization, were deeply rooted in the nation's history and identity, and the consequences of the war were far-reaching and profound. The Civil War transformed the United States politically, socially, and economically, leading to the abolition of slavery, the expansion of civil rights, and the reshaping of American society. While the scars of the war have not fully healed, its legacy serves as a reminder of the enduring struggle for freedom, equality, and justice that continues to animate the American experience.

Chapter 8: Reconstruction

Reconstruction was a transformative period in American history, lasting from 1865 to 1877, during which the United States sought to rebuild the South, integrate freed slaves into society, and redefine the meaning of freedom and citizenship in the aftermath of the Civil War. In this chapter, we will explore the efforts to rebuild the South and integrate freed slaves into society, the rise of Jim Crow laws and the struggle for civil rights, and the disputed legacy of Reconstruction.

Efforts to Rebuild the South and Integrate Freed Slaves into Society

Reconstruction Amendments

One of the central goals of Reconstruction was to secure the rights and freedoms of formerly enslaved Africans and ensure their full participation in American society. To achieve this goal, Congress passed a series of constitutional amendments known as the Reconstruction Amendments. The 13th Amendment, ratified in 1865, abolished slavery throughout the United States, while the 14th Amendment, ratified in 1868, granted citizenship and equal protection under the law to all persons born or naturalized in the United States. The 15th Amendment, ratified in 1870, prohibited the denial of voting rights based on race, color, or previous condition of servitude.

Freedmen's Bureau

To assist newly emancipated Africans in the transition to freedom, Congress established the Freedmen's Bureau in 1865. The Freedmen's Bureau provided food, clothing, education, and legal assistance to freed slaves and impoverished whites in the South. The bureau also helped to settle disputes between landowners and former slaves, oversee labor contracts, and establish schools and hospitals for freedmen and their families. Despite its efforts, the Freedmen's Bureau faced opposition from white Southerners and limited resources from the federal government, hindering its effectiveness in achieving its goals.

Reconstruction Governments

During Reconstruction, the federal government imposed military rule on the former Confederate states and established new governments based on universal male suffrage and African American participation. These Reconstruction governments, often led by Republican coalitions of Northerners and Southern whites known as "carpetbaggers" and African Americans known as "scalawags," sought to implement social, political, and economic reforms aimed at promoting equality and justice. The Reconstruction governments enacted civil rights legislation, established public schools, and promoted economic development through infrastructure projects such as roads, railroads, and public works programs.

Land Redistribution and Civil Rights

One of the most contentious issues during Reconstruction was the question of land redistribution and economic justice for formerly enslaved Africans. Some Radical Republicans advocated for the redistribution of land to freed slaves as a means of achieving economic independence and social equality. However, efforts to redistribute land were met with resistance from white landowners and conservative politicians who sought to preserve the plantation system and maintain white supremacy in the South. As a result, land redistribution efforts were largely unsuccessful, and many freedmen remained economically dependent on their former masters or became sharecroppers or tenant farmers.

The Rise of Jim Crow Laws and the Struggle for Civil Rights

Reconstruction Backlash

The gains made during Reconstruction were short-lived, as white Southerners quickly sought to undermine the rights and freedoms of African Americans and restore white supremacy in the South. The Reconstruction governments faced opposition from white supremacist organizations such as the Ku Klux Klan, which used violence, intimidation, and terror tactics to intimidate and disenfranchise African Americans and their allies. The Compromise of 1877, which ended Reconstruction and withdrew federal troops from the South, paved the way for the rise of Jim Crow laws and the imposition of segregation and racial discrimination in the region.

Jim Crow Laws

Jim Crow laws were a series of state and local laws enacted in the Southern states between the late 19th and early 20th centuries that enforced racial segregation and discrimination. These laws mandated separate facilities and services for African Americans and whites in public spaces such as schools, parks, restaurants, theaters, and transportation. Jim Crow laws also restricted African American voting rights through poll taxes, literacy tests, and other discriminatory measures designed to disenfranchise black voters and perpetuate white supremacy. The legal doctrine of "separate but equal," established by the Supreme Court in Plessy v. Ferguson (1896), upheld the constitutionality of segregation and institutionalized racial inequality in America for decades.

Civil Rights Movement

Despite the oppressive conditions of segregation and discrimination, African Americans in the South and their allies in the North resisted Jim Crow laws and fought for civil rights and racial equality. The Civil Rights Movement, which emerged in the late 19th and early 20th centuries, was a grassroots movement led by activists, organizers, and community leaders who challenged segregation, discrimination, and injustice through nonviolent protest, legal action, and political mobilization. Figures such as Booker T. Washington, W.E.B. Du Bois, Ida B. Wells, and Mary Church Terrell played key roles in the fight for civil rights, advocating for social and economic equality, educational opportunities, and political empowerment for African Americans.

Legal Challenges and Supreme Court Decisions

The struggle for civil rights also took place in the courts, where African American lawyers and civil rights organizations challenged the constitutionality of segregation and discrimination. In landmark cases such as Brown v. Board of Education (1954), which declared segregation in public schools unconstitutional, and Shelley v. Kraemer (1948), which struck down racially restrictive housing covenants, the Supreme Court played a crucial role in dismantling the legal framework of Jim Crow and advancing the cause of civil rights in America. However, the implementation of court decisions often met with resistance from white supremacist politicians and segregationists, leading to protracted legal battles and ongoing struggles for equality and justice.

The Disputed Legacy of Reconstruction

Interpretations of Reconstruction

The legacy of Reconstruction remains a subject of debate and controversy in American historiography. For many years, Reconstruction was portrayed as a period of corruption, misrule, and failure, characterized by Northern carpetbaggers and Southern scalawags who exploited the South for their own gain. This "Lost Cause" interpretation of Reconstruction, propagated by white supremacist historians and Confederate sympathizers, sought to justify the overthrow of Reconstruction governments and the imposition of Jim Crow laws as necessary measures to restore order and protect Southern civilization.

Revisionist Interpretations

In recent decades, scholars have challenged the traditional interpretation of Reconstruction and offered new perspectives on the era. Revisionist historians have emphasized the achievements of Reconstruction, including the establishment of public education, the expansion of civil rights and political participation, and the emergence of a new vision of American citizenship based on equality and justice. Revisionist interpretations have highlighted the resilience and agency of African Americans during Reconstruction and the lasting impact of the era on American society and politics.

Legacies of Reconstruction

Despite its contested legacy, Reconstruction had profound and lasting consequences for American society. The era marked a period of transition from slavery to freedom, from feudalism to democracy, and from the Old South to the New South. Reconstruction laid the foundation for the modern civil rights movement and the ongoing struggle for racial equality and justice in America. The legacy of Reconstruction serves as a reminder of the unfinished work of democracy and the enduring quest for freedom and equality in the United States.

Chapter 9: Industrialization and Urbanization

The late 19th and early 20th centuries witnessed a profound transformation of American society as the nation underwent rapid industrialization and urbanization. During this period, the United States transitioned from an agrarian economy to an industrial powerhouse, with vast implications for the economy, society, and politics. In this chapter, we will explore the rise of industry and its impact on American society, immigration and the growth of cities, and the labor movements and the fight for workers' rights that emerged in response to the challenges of industrialization.

The Rise of Industry and Its Impact on American Society

Industrial Revolution

The Industrial Revolution, which began in Britain in the late 18th century and spread to the United States in the early 19th century, transformed the American economy and society. The development of new technologies, such as the steam engine, the cotton gin, and the telegraph, revolutionized manufacturing, transportation, and communication, leading to the rise of factories, railroads, and urban centers. The Industrial Revolution spurred economic growth, urbanization, and social change, as traditional agrarian societies gave way to modern industrial societies.

Growth of Industry

The late 19th century saw the rapid expansion of industry in the United States, fueled by technological innovation, natural resources, and a growing market for manufactured goods. Industries such as steel, oil, railroads, textiles, and machinery emerged as leading sectors of the economy, driving economic development and creating new opportunities for investment, entrepreneurship, and wealth creation. Industrial tycoons such as Andrew Carnegie, John D. Rockefeller, and J.P. Morgan amassed vast fortunes and wielded immense power and influence over the nation's economy and politics.

Impact on American Society

The rise of industry had far-reaching implications for American society, transforming the way people lived, worked, and interacted with one another. Industrialization led to urbanization, as rural populations migrated to cities in search of employment and opportunity. The growth of cities fueled the demand for housing, infrastructure, and public services, leading to the development of new neighborhoods, suburbs, and urban amenities. Industrialization also brought about social changes, as traditional social hierarchies gave way to new forms of social organization based on class, ethnicity, and occupation.

Social Stratification

Industrialization led to the emergence of a new social order characterized by growing disparities of wealth and power. While industrialization created new opportunities for upward mobility and economic advancement, it also widened the gap between the rich and the poor, leading to social stratification and class conflict. The industrial workforce was divided into distinct social classes, including wealthy industrialists, middle-class professionals and managers, and a growing working class of factory workers, laborers, and immigrants who toiled in harsh and dangerous conditions for low wages and long hours.

Immigration and the Growth of Cities

Immigration Trends

The late 19th and early 20th centuries saw a massive influx of immigrants to the United States, driven by economic hardship, political instability, and social upheaval in Europe and other parts of the world. Immigrants from countries such as Ireland, Germany, Italy, Russia, and Eastern Europe arrived in search of opportunity and freedom in America, drawn by the promise of jobs, land, and a better life for themselves and their families. The United States became a melting pot of cultures, languages, and traditions, as immigrants settled in cities and towns across the country and contributed to the nation's economic and cultural diversity.

Urban Growth

The influx of immigrants fueled the growth of cities and the expansion of urban areas, as new arrivals settled in immigrant enclaves and industrial centers. Cities such as New York, Chicago, Philadelphia, Boston, and Detroit experienced explosive population growth, as immigrants flocked to urban areas in search of employment in factories, mills, mines, and construction projects. The growth of cities led to overcrowding, congestion, and social problems such as poverty, crime, and disease, as urban infrastructure struggled to keep pace with the demands of rapid urbanization.

Ethnic Neighborhoods

Immigrants often settled in ethnic neighborhoods or enclaves, where they could find support, solidarity, and familiarity in a foreign land. These ethnic neighborhoods, such as New York's Lower East Side, Chicago's Little Italy, and San Francisco's Chinatown, became vibrant centers of immigrant life, culture, and community, where residents maintained their customs, traditions, and languages while adapting to the demands of urban life. Ethnic neighborhoods were also sites of social and political activism, as immigrants organized mutual aid societies, labor unions, and political clubs to advocate for their rights and interests.

Labor Movements and the Fight for Workers' Rights

Working Conditions

The growth of industry and urbanization brought about profound changes in the nature of work and labor relations in America. Factory workers, miners, railroad workers, and other industrial laborers faced harsh and often dangerous working conditions, including long hours, low wages, and unsafe workplaces. Workers were subject to exploitation, abuse, and discrimination by employers who sought to maximize profits at the expense of their employees' health, safety, and well-being.

Rise of Labor Unions

In response to the challenges of industrialization and urbanization, workers began to organize and mobilize to improve their working conditions and secure their rights. Labor unions emerged as powerful advocates for workers' rights, organizing strikes, boycotts, and collective bargaining efforts to demand higher wages, shorter hours, and safer working conditions. The Knights of Labor, founded in 1869, and the American Federation of Labor (AFL), founded in 1886, were among the leading labor organizations of the late 19th century, representing millions of workers in a variety of industries.

Strikes and Labor Struggles

The late 19th and early 20th centuries were marked by numerous strikes, labor disputes, and industrial conflicts as workers fought to assert their rights and improve their conditions. Some of the most notable labor struggles of the period include the Haymarket Affair (1886), the Homestead Strike (1892), and the Pullman Strike (1894), which saw violent clashes between workers, employers, and law enforcement agencies. These strikes and labor struggles galvanized public opinion, raised awareness of labor issues, and ultimately led to significant gains for workers in terms of wages, hours, and workplace safety.

Government Regulation

The labor movements of the late 19th and early 20th centuries also led to increased government intervention in labor relations and the passage of labor laws aimed at protecting workers' rights and regulating the behavior of employers. The Fair Labor Standards Act of 1938, for example, established a minimum wage, maximum hours, and overtime pay for workers in certain industries, while the National Labor Relations Act of 1935, also known as the Wagner Act, guaranteed workers the right to organize and bargain collectively with their employers.

Conclusion

The period of industrialization and urbanization in the late 19th and early 20th centuries was a time of profound change and transformation in American society, as the nation transitioned from an agrarian economy to an industrial powerhouse. The rise of industry and the growth of cities reshaped the economic, social, and political landscape of the United States, leading to both opportunities and challenges for American workers and society as a whole.

Chapter 10: The Progressive Era

The Progressive Era, spanning roughly from the late 19th century to the early 20th century, was a period of social, political, and economic reform in the United States. Fueled by concerns about the negative effects of industrialization, urbanization, and political corruption, progressives sought to address the problems of poverty, inequality, and injustice through government intervention and social activism. In this chapter, we will explore the efforts to address social and political reform, the fight against corruption and the influence of muckrakers, and the passage of progressive legislation and the rise of Theodore Roosevelt.

Efforts to Address Social and Political Reform

Social Welfare Reforms

The Progressive Era saw a wave of social welfare reforms aimed at improving the lives of the nation's most vulnerable citizens. Progressive reformers advocated for government intervention to address the social and economic problems caused by industrialization and urbanization, including poverty, unemployment, and unsafe working conditions. Social welfare programs such as child labor laws, minimum wage laws, and workplace safety regulations were enacted to protect workers and improve their living and working conditions. Progressives also championed the cause of social justice, advocating for women's suffrage, civil rights, and public health reforms to promote the well-being of all Americans.

Education Reforms

Education reform was another key priority for progressives, who viewed education as a means of promoting social mobility and democratic citizenship. Progressive educators such as John Dewey emphasized the importance of experiential learning, critical thinking, and civic engagement in the classroom, advocating for a more child-centered and holistic approach to education. Progressive reforms led to the expansion of public education, the establishment of kindergarten programs, and the implementation of curriculum reforms designed to prepare students for the challenges of the modern world.

Political Reforms

Progressives also sought to reform the political system to make it more responsive to the needs and interests of the American people. Political reforms such as the direct primary, the initiative, the referendum, and the recall were introduced to increase citizen participation in the democratic process and hold elected officials accountable to the public. Progressives also advocated for the regulation of political campaign financing, the direct election of senators, and the establishment of nonpartisan civil service systems to combat political corruption and patronage.

The Fight Against Corruption and the Influence of Muckrakers

Political Corruption

Political corruption was rampant during the Gilded Age, as powerful industrialists and political machines wielded immense power and influence over the nation's politics and economy. The spoils system, in which political favors and government jobs were exchanged for political support, fueled corruption and patronage at all levels of government. Progressive reformers, outraged by the excesses of the Gilded Age, sought to root out corruption and restore integrity and accountability to government through a series of political reforms and anti-corruption measures.

Muckrakers

Muckrakers were investigative journalists and writers who exposed corruption, abuse, and injustice in American society through their investigative reporting and exposés. Muckrakers such as Ida Tarbell, Upton Sinclair, Lincoln Steffens, and Jacob Riis shone a spotlight on the dark underbelly of the Gilded Age, revealing the unsavory practices of monopolistic trusts, unscrupulous business practices, and political corruption. Their exposés, published in popular magazines such as McClure's, Collier's, and The Nation, helped to galvanize public opinion and mobilize support for progressive reforms.

The Role of Muckrakers

Muckrakers played a crucial role in the Progressive Era by raising awareness of social and political problems and mobilizing public support for reform. Their exposés helped to expose the abuses of industrial capitalism, spark public outrage, and pressure politicians to take action to address the nation's most pressing problems. Muckrakers were instrumental in exposing corruption in government, business, and society and paving the way for the passage of progressive legislation to reform the nation's institutions and promote the public good.

The Passage of Progressive Legislation and the Rise of Theodore Roosevelt

Progressive Legislation

The Progressive Era saw the passage of a wide range of progressive legislation aimed at addressing the social, economic, and political problems of the day. Progressive reforms such as the Pure Food and Drug Act (1906), the Meat Inspection Act (1906), and the Federal Reserve Act (1913) were enacted to protect consumers, regulate industry, and promote economic stability. Other progressive reforms included the Clayton Antitrust Act (1914), which strengthened antitrust laws to curb the power of monopolistic trusts, and the Federal Trade Commission Act (1914), which established the Federal Trade Commission to enforce antitrust laws and protect consumers from unfair business practices.

The Rise of Theodore Roosevelt

Theodore Roosevelt, who served as President of the United States from 1901 to 1909, was a central figure in the Progressive Era and a champion of progressive reform. Known for his energetic leadership and reformist agenda, Roosevelt advocated for a "Square Deal" for all Americans, which included measures to regulate big business, protect consumers, and conserve natural resources. Roosevelt took on powerful corporate interests such as the trusts and monopolies, using the power of the federal government to break up monopolistic practices and promote competition in the marketplace. Roosevelt's leadership and reformist agenda helped to usher in a new era of progressive reform and activism in American politics, laying the groundwork for the reforms of the Progressive Era and shaping the course of American history for decades to come.

Conclusion

The Progressive Era was a time of sweeping social, political, and economic reform in the United States, as progressives sought to address the problems of industrialization, urbanization, and political corruption through government intervention and social activism. Efforts to address social and political reform led to the passage of progressive legislation aimed at improving the lives of the nation's citizens and promoting the public good. The fight against corruption and the influence of muckrakers played a crucial role in raising awareness of social and political problems and mobilizing public support for reform. The rise of Theodore Roosevelt as a champion of progressive reform helped to galvanize public opinion and push forward the progressive agenda, paving the way for the reforms of the Progressive Era and shaping the course of American history for generations to come.

Chapter 11: America in World War I

World War I, also known as the Great War, was a global conflict that took place from 1914 to 1918, involving many of the world's great powers. For the United States, World War I represented a significant departure from its traditional policy of neutrality and isolationism, thrusting the nation onto the world stage as a major player in international affairs. In this chapter, we will explore the causes of World War I and America's entry into the conflict, the home front and the impact of the war on American society, and the Treaty of Versailles and the League of Nations.

Causes of World War I and America's Entry into the Conflict

Militarism and Alliances

The causes of World War I were complex and multifaceted, rooted in a combination of long-term structural factors and short-term triggers. One of the key causes of the war was the system of militarism and alliances that characterized European politics in the late 19th and early 20th centuries. The major powers of Europe had formed a series of alliances and ententes, creating a complex web of diplomatic commitments and mutual defense agreements that heightened tensions and increased the likelihood of conflict.

Imperialism and Colonial Rivalries

Another cause of World War I was the competition among the great powers for colonies and territories around the world. The age of imperialism had led to the expansion of European empires in Africa, Asia, and the Americas, creating rivalries and conflicts over territory, resources, and influence. The scramble for colonies exacerbated tensions between the major powers and contributed to the outbreak of war in Europe.

Nationalism and Ethnic Tensions

Nationalism and ethnic tensions were also significant factors in the outbreak of World War I. The rise of nationalism and the desire for self-determination among ethnic and national groups in Europe led to conflicts and tensions within the multinational empires of Austria-Hungary, Russia, and the Ottoman Empire. The assassination of Archduke Franz Ferdinand of Austria-Hungary in Sarajevo in 1914, by a Bosnian Serb nationalist, sparked a chain reaction of events that ultimately led to the outbreak of war.

America's Entry into the War

When World War I broke out in Europe in 1914, the United States initially pursued a policy of neutrality and non-intervention, seeking to avoid becoming entangled in the conflict. However, as the war dragged on and the situation in Europe deteriorated, America's stance towards the conflict began to change. Several factors contributed to America's eventual entry into the war in 1917:

1. Unrestricted Submarine Warfare: The German policy of unrestricted submarine warfare, which targeted civilian ships and neutral vessels, including American merchant ships, led to the loss of American lives and property and provoked outrage in the United States.

2. The Zimmerman Telegram: In 1917, the British intercepted a secret telegram from the German government to Mexico, proposing a military alliance against the United States in exchange for the return of territory lost in the Mexican-American War. The revelation of the Zimmerman Telegram further inflamed anti-German sentiment in the United States and contributed to the decision to enter the war.

3. Idealism and Wilson's Vision: President Woodrow Wilson, who was re-elected in 1916 on a platform of peace and neutrality, gradually came to believe that American intervention was necessary to "make the world safe for democracy" and promote peace and justice on the world stage.

4. Economic Interests: American economic interests, including trade with the Allied powers and loans to European governments, also played a role in America's decision to enter the war. The prospect of lucrative wartime contracts and economic opportunities influenced public opinion and political decision-making in favor of intervention.

The Home Front and the Impact of the War on American Society

Mobilization and War Effort

With America's entry into World War I in 1917, the nation mobilized for war on an unprecedented scale. The federal government, under the leadership of President Woodrow Wilson, undertook a massive mobilization effort to raise, train, and equip a large army, navy, and air force to fight in Europe. The Selective Service Act of 1917 authorized the draft of millions of young men into the military, while the War Industries Board coordinated the production and distribution of war materiel and resources to support the war effort.

War Propaganda and Public Opinion

War propaganda played a crucial role in shaping public opinion and rallying support for the war effort. The Committee on Public Information, headed by journalist George Creel, launched a massive propaganda campaign to promote patriotism, support for the war, and hostility towards the enemy. Propaganda posters, films, newspapers, and speeches depicted Germans as barbaric Huns and portrayed the war as a noble crusade for freedom and democracy. The propaganda campaign succeeded in mobilizing public support for the war and suppressing dissent and opposition to the government's war policies.

Social Changes and Cultural Shifts

The war had profound social and cultural impacts on American society, transforming the lives of millions of Americans in both positive and negative ways. The war brought about significant demographic changes as millions of young men enlisted or were drafted into the military, leaving behind families, communities, and jobs. Women entered the workforce in large numbers to fill the vacancies left by men serving in the military, taking on jobs in factories, offices, and other traditionally male-dominated industries. The war also accelerated the process of urbanization and industrialization, as cities and industries expanded to meet the demands of wartime production and mobilization.

Civil Liberties and Civil Rights

The war also had implications for civil liberties and civil rights in the United States. In the name of national security and wartime necessity, the government imposed restrictions on freedom of speech, press, and assembly, leading to the suppression of dissent and opposition to the war. The Espionage Act of 1917 and the Sedition Act of 1918 authorized the government to prosecute individuals who spoke out against the war or the government's war policies, leading to the arrest and imprisonment of anti-war activists, socialists, and anarchists. African Americans and other minority groups faced discrimination and segregation in the military and in society, despite their contributions to the war effort.

The Treaty of Versailles and the League of Nations

Peace Negotiations

As the war drew to a close in 1918, the victorious Allied powers began negotiations to determine the terms of peace and to address the causes of the conflict. The Treaty of Versailles, signed in 1919, imposed harsh penalties and reparations on Germany, including territorial losses, military restrictions, and financial obligations, which many historians argue contributed to the rise of Adolf Hitler and the outbreak of World War II.

The League of Nations

One of the key provisions of the Treaty of Versailles was the establishment of the League of Nations, an international organization founded to promote peace, security, and cooperation among nations and to prevent future conflicts. The League of Nations represented a bold experiment in international diplomacy and collective security, but it ultimately failed to prevent the outbreak of World War II due to a lack of enforcement mechanisms and the refusal of major powers such as the United States to join or participate fully in the organization.

America's Role

Despite President Woodrow Wilson's advocacy for the League of Nations and his efforts to promote international cooperation and collective security, the United

States ultimately failed to ratify the Treaty of Versailles or join the League of Nations. The Senate's rejection of the treaty and America's retreat into isolationism and disengagement from international affairs marked a significant turning point in American foreign policy, as the nation returned to a policy of isolationism and non-intervention in world affairs.

Conclusion

America's involvement in World War I represented a watershed moment in the nation's history, marking its emergence as a global power and reshaping its role in international affairs. The war had profound impacts on American society, politics, and culture, transforming the lives of millions of Americans and shaping the course of the 20th century. The war brought about significant social and economic changes, accelerating the process of urbanization, industrialization, and social reform, while also leading to restrictions on civil liberties and civil rights in the name of national security. The war also had far-reaching consequences for the international order, leading to the collapse of empires, the redrawing of borders, and the establishment of new nation-states in Europe and the Middle East.

The Treaty of Versailles and the League of Nations represented attempts to address the causes of the war and promote peace and stability in the aftermath of the conflict, but ultimately failed to prevent the outbreak of another world war. America's rejection of the treaty and the League of Nations reflected a growing disillusionment with international diplomacy and a return to isolationism and non-intervention in world affairs. However, America's experience in World War I laid the groundwork for its emergence as a global superpower in the 20th century, shaping its role in world politics and setting the stage for its future leadership on the world stage.

Chapter 12: The Roaring Twenties

The Roaring Twenties, also known as the Jazz Age, was a period of cultural, social, and economic dynamism in the United States that spanned from the end of World War I in 1918 to the onset of the Great Depression in 1929. The decade was characterized by rapid technological advancements, urbanization, and unprecedented prosperity, as well as profound social and cultural changes that transformed American society. In this chapter, we will explore the Jazz Age and cultural changes in America, the impact of prohibition and the rise of organized crime, and the Wall Street Crash of 1929 and the onset of the Great Depression.

The Jazz Age and Cultural Changes in America

The Rise of Jazz

The Roaring Twenties saw the emergence of jazz music as a dominant cultural force in America. Originating in African American communities in New Orleans and other urban centers, jazz music combined elements of African rhythms, blues, ragtime, and European musical traditions to create a vibrant and distinctive musical style. Jazz became synonymous with the spirit of the Roaring Twenties, embodying the energy, excitement, and liberation of the era. Jazz clubs and speakeasies proliferated in cities such as New York, Chicago, and Harlem, where musicians such as Louis Armstrong, Duke Ellington, and Bessie Smith performed to enthusiastic audiences.

The Harlem Renaissance

The Roaring Twenties also witnessed the flowering of African American culture and art known as the Harlem Renaissance. Centered in the Harlem neighborhood of New York City, the Harlem Renaissance was a cultural and intellectual movement that celebrated the achievements of African American writers, artists, musicians, and intellectuals. Writers such as Langston Hughes, Zora Neale Hurston, and Claude McKay produced works that explored themes of race, identity, and the African American experience, while artists such as

Aaron Douglas and Romare Bearden created vibrant visual representations of African American life and culture.

Changing Social Norms

The Roaring Twenties brought about significant changes in social norms and attitudes towards gender, sexuality, and morality. The decade witnessed the rise of the "New Woman," who challenged traditional gender roles and expectations by asserting her independence, pursuing higher education and careers, and participating in the social and cultural life of the city. Flappers, young women who embraced a liberated and carefree lifestyle, became icons of the Jazz Age, challenging conventions of dress, behavior, and morality with their bobbed hair, short skirts, and rebellious attitudes.

Technological Innovations

The Roaring Twenties were also a time of rapid technological advancements and innovations that revolutionized everyday life. The widespread adoption of electricity, automobiles, telephones, and other modern conveniences transformed the way people lived, worked, and socialized, leading to increased mobility, connectivity, and consumerism. The proliferation of new technologies and mass media, including radio, motion pictures, and mass-produced magazines, contributed to the spread of popular culture and the creation of a shared national identity.

The Impact of Prohibition and the Rise of Organized Crime

Prohibition

One of the defining features of the Roaring Twenties was the nationwide prohibition of alcohol, enacted through the 18th Amendment to the Constitution in 1919 and enforced by the Volstead Act. Prohibition was intended to curb alcohol consumption and reduce social problems such as crime, poverty, and domestic violence, but it had unintended consequences that fueled the rise of organized crime and corruption. Speakeasies, illegal bars, and underground clubs proliferated across the country, catering to the demand for alcohol and providing opportunities for bootleggers, gangsters, and organized crime syndicates to profit from the illegal liquor trade.

Rise of Organized Crime

The era of prohibition gave rise to powerful criminal organizations such as the Chicago Outfit, the Five Families of New York, and the Detroit Partnership, which controlled the production, distribution, and sale of illegal alcohol through violence, intimidation, and corruption. Gangsters such as Al Capone, Lucky Luciano, and Bugsy Siegel became notorious figures in American popular culture, glamorized in the media as larger-than-life antiheroes and symbols of rebellion against authority. The profits from the illegal liquor trade fueled the growth of organized crime and contributed to the escalation of violence and lawlessness in American cities.

Law Enforcement and Corruption

Prohibition also led to widespread corruption and lawlessness within law enforcement agencies and government institutions. Prohibition agents, police officers, and public officials were often bribed or coerced into turning a blind eye to the activities of bootleggers and speakeasies, while others actively colluded with organized crime syndicates in exchange for money, favors, or political support. The failure of prohibition to achieve its intended goals, coupled with the widespread public defiance of the law, ultimately led to its repeal in 1933 with the passage of the 21st Amendment.

The Wall Street Crash of 1929 and the Onset of the Great Depression

Economic Boom and Bust

The Roaring Twenties were a time of unprecedented economic prosperity and growth, fueled by technological innovation, industrial expansion, and consumer spending. The stock market soared to new heights, as investors flocked to buy shares in the booming industries of the day, such as automobiles, radio, and aviation. However, beneath the surface of this economic prosperity lurked fundamental weaknesses and imbalances that would ultimately lead to the collapse of the stock market and the onset of the Great Depression.

Stock Market Speculation

One of the key factors that contributed to the Wall Street Crash of 1929 was the widespread speculation and overvaluation of stocks in the stock market. Investors, emboldened by the prospect of easy profits and fueled by speculation and greed, engaged in risky and speculative trading practices, such as buying stocks on margin and investing in speculative "blue sky" ventures. The stock market became increasingly disconnected from the underlying fundamentals of the economy, creating a speculative bubble that was ripe for collapse.

Black Thursday and the Crash

The stock market bubble finally burst on October 24, 1929, a day that would come to be known as "Black Thursday." Panicked investors rushed to sell their stocks in a frantic attempt to salvage their investments, leading to a massive sell-off and a precipitous decline in stock prices. The following week, on "Black Tuesday," October 29, 1929, the stock market crashed, with the Dow Jones Industrial Average plunging by over 25% in a single day, wiping out billions of dollars in wealth and triggering a financial panic.

Economic Consequences

The Wall Street Crash of 1929 marked the beginning of the Great Depression, the most severe economic downturn in modern history. The collapse of the stock market sent shockwaves throughout the economy, leading to widespread bank failures, business closures, and mass unemployment. Millions of Americans lost their jobs, their homes, and their savings, as the economy spiraled into a deep and prolonged recession. The Great Depression would have profound and far-reaching consequences for American society, politics, and culture, shaping the course of the 20th century and leaving an indelible mark on the nation's collective memory.

Conclusion

The Roaring Twenties was a time of unprecedented social, cultural, and economic change in America, characterized by rapid technological advancements, urbanization, and prosperity. The Jazz Age brought about a cultural renaissance that celebrated the vitality and creativity of American life, while prohibition and the rise of organized crime revealed the darker side of the era's excesses and contradictions. The Wall Street Crash of 1929, however, served as a harsh reality check, bringing an abrupt end to the decade of prosperity and ushering in a period of economic hardship and social upheaval.

Chapter 13: The New Deal

The New Deal, implemented by President Franklin D. Roosevelt in response to the Great Depression, represented a bold and sweeping series of government programs and reforms aimed at providing relief, recovery, and reform to the American people. Launched in the midst of the worst economic crisis in the nation's history, the New Deal transformed the role of the federal government in American society and laid the groundwork for the modern welfare state. In this chapter, we will explore Franklin D. Roosevelt's response to the Great Depression, the expansion of government programs and reforms under the New Deal, and the legacy of the New Deal in shaping modern America.

Franklin D. Roosevelt's Response to the Great Depression

Inaugural Address and the First Hundred Days

Upon assuming office in March 1933, President Franklin D. Roosevelt wasted no time in taking action to address the nation's economic crisis. In his inaugural address, Roosevelt famously declared, "The only thing we have to fear is fear itself," and pledged to take bold and decisive action to combat the Great Depression. In the first hundred days of his administration, Roosevelt launched an unprecedented flurry of legislative activity, sending a series of bills to Congress aimed at providing immediate relief to the millions of Americans suffering from unemployment, poverty, and despair.

The Three R's: Relief, Recovery, Reform

Roosevelt's response to the Great Depression was guided by the principles of relief, recovery, and reform, which became known as the "Three R's" of the New Deal. Relief programs were aimed at providing immediate assistance to those in need, including direct relief payments, food assistance, and job creation programs such as the Civilian Conservation Corps (CCC) and the Works Progress Administration (WPA). Recovery programs focused on stimulating economic growth and restoring confidence in the economy through measures such as public works projects, agricultural subsidies, and financial reforms. Reform programs sought to address the underlying causes of the Great Depression and prevent future economic crises through measures such as banking reform, regulation of the stock market, and the creation of social safety net programs such as Social Security.

The Expansion of Government Programs and Reforms

The First New Deal

The First New Deal, implemented during Roosevelt's first term in office from 1933 to 1935, focused on providing immediate relief and recovery to the American people. One of the first measures enacted by Roosevelt was the Emergency Banking Act of 1933, which declared a national bank holiday and authorized the federal government to reorganize and stabilize the nation's banking system. This was followed by the passage of the Glass-Steagall Act, which established the Federal Deposit Insurance Corporation (FDIC) to insure bank deposits and prevent future bank failures.

The Second New Deal

The Second New Deal, implemented during Roosevelt's second term in office from 1935 to 1939, built upon the achievements of the First New Deal and focused on more ambitious reforms and social welfare programs. One of the key initiatives of the Second New Deal was the passage of the Social Security Act of 1935, which established a system of old-age pensions, unemployment insurance, and assistance for the disabled and disadvantaged. Other important measures included the National Labor Relations Act (also known as the Wagner Act), which guaranteed workers the right to organize and bargain collectively, and the Fair Labor Standards Act, which established a federal minimum wage and maximum workweek.

Alphabet Agencies

The New Deal also created a multitude of federal agencies and programs, collectively known as the "alphabet agencies," to administer and implement its various relief, recovery, and reform measures. These agencies included the Civil Works Administration (CWA), the Public Works Administration (PWA), the Tennessee Valley Authority (TVA), and the Agricultural Adjustment Administration (AAA), among others. These agencies employed millions of Americans in public works projects, infrastructure improvements, and conservation efforts, providing much-needed jobs and economic stimulus during the Great Depression.

The Legacy of the New Deal in Shaping Modern America

Economic Recovery and Social Welfare

The New Deal is widely credited with helping to alleviate the worst effects of the Great Depression and lay the foundation for the nation's eventual recovery. The New Deal's relief and recovery programs provided immediate assistance to millions of Americans in need, while its reforms and regulations helped to stabilize the economy and prevent future economic crises. The Social Security Act, in particular, represented a landmark achievement in the establishment of a social safety net for the American people, providing financial security and assistance to millions of elderly, disabled, and unemployed Americans.

Expansion of the Federal Government

The New Deal also expanded the role of the federal government in American society, ushering in an era of increased government intervention and regulation of the economy. The creation of federal agencies and programs to administer relief, recovery, and reform measures marked a significant expansion of the federal bureaucracy and laid the groundwork for the modern welfare state. The New Deal's legacy can be seen in the continued presence of federal agencies such as the Social Security Administration, the Federal Deposit Insurance Corporation, and the Securities and Exchange Commission, which continue to play vital roles in regulating and administering social welfare programs and financial markets.

Transformation of American Politics

The New Deal transformed the political landscape of the United States, realigning the Democratic Party's base of support and reshaping the relationship between the government and the American people. Roosevelt's coalition of urban workers, farmers, minorities, and progressives formed the backbone of the New Deal coalition, which dominated American politics for decades and laid the groundwork for the expansion of the welfare state and the enactment of further social and economic reforms in the decades that followed. The New Deal's emphasis on government intervention and social welfare also contributed to the emergence of a more activist role for government in addressing social and economic problems, shaping the contours of American politics and policy for generations to come.

Conclusion

The New Deal represented a watershed moment in American history, as President Franklin D. Roosevelt and his administration responded to the unprecedented challenges of the Great Depression with bold and innovative measures aimed at providing relief, recovery, and reform to the American people. The New Deal's legacy can be seen in the expansion of the federal government, the establishment of a social safety net, and the transformation of American politics and society. While the New Deal did not solve all of the nation's problems, it laid the groundwork for the modern welfare state and left an indelible mark on the nation's collective memory as a symbol of government action in times of crisis.

Chapter 14: America in World War II

World War II was a global conflict that engulfed much of the world from 1939 to 1945, pitting the Allied powers, including the United States, against the Axis powers, led by Nazi Germany, Imperial Japan, and Fascist Italy. America's entry into World War II marked a turning point in the conflict and had profound implications for the outcome of the war and the course of world history. In this chapter, we will explore the attack on Pearl Harbor and America's entry into World War II, the home front and the mobilization of industry, and key battles and turning points in the war.

The Attack on Pearl Harbor and America's Entry into World War II

Road to War

In the years leading up to World War II, tensions between the United States and Japan had been escalating over Japan's aggressive expansionism in East Asia and the Pacific. The United States had imposed economic sanctions on Japan in response to its invasion of China and its expansionist policies in the Pacific. In September 1940, the United States passed the Export Control Act, which restricted the sale of oil and other strategic resources to Japan, further exacerbating tensions between the two nations.

Pearl Harbor

On the morning of December 7, 1941, the Imperial Japanese Navy launched a surprise attack on the United States Pacific Fleet stationed at Pearl Harbor, Hawaii. The attack, which caught the American forces completely off guard, resulted in the loss of over 2,400 American lives and inflicted severe damage on the Pacific Fleet, including the sinking or disabling of eight battleships and the destruction of over 200 aircraft. The attack on Pearl Harbor shocked the American public and propelled the United States into World War II, as President Franklin D. Roosevelt famously described December 7, 1941, as "a date which will live in infamy."

America's Entry into World War II

In the wake of the attack on Pearl Harbor, President Roosevelt addressed a joint session of Congress and called for a declaration of war against Japan. The following day, on December 8, 1941, Congress overwhelmingly voted to declare war on Japan, with only one dissenting vote. Three days later, on December 11, 1941, Germany and Italy, Japan's allies, declared war on the United States, leading to America's entry into World War II on the side of the Allied powers.

The Home Front and the Mobilization of Industry

War Production

America's entry into World War II sparked a massive mobilization effort on the home front to support the war effort. The American economy was transformed virtually overnight, as factories and industries were converted to produce war materiel and supplies for the military. The War Production Board, established by President Roosevelt in 1942, coordinated the production and distribution of war goods, prioritizing the production of tanks, planes, ships, and munitions needed to support the Allied war effort.

Rationing and Sacrifice

The war also brought about significant changes in daily life on the home front, as Americans were called upon to make sacrifices and ration their consumption of essential goods and resources. The Office of Price Administration (OPA) implemented rationing programs to conserve scarce resources such as rubber, gasoline, food, and clothing, while also regulating prices and wages to prevent inflation and ensure fairness in the distribution of goods. Americans were issued ration books and ration stamps, which limited the amount of goods they could purchase and consume, leading to changes in dietary habits, transportation patterns, and lifestyle choices.

Women in the Workforce

The war also brought about profound changes in the American workforce, as millions of men enlisted or were drafted into the military, leaving behind vacancies in factories, offices, and other workplaces. To fill the labor shortages, women entered the workforce in unprecedented numbers, taking on jobs traditionally held by men in industries such as manufacturing, construction, and transportation. The iconic image of "Rosie the Riveter" symbolized the contribution of women to the war effort and the vital role they played in supporting the American war machine.

Key Battles and Turning Points in the War

Battle of Midway

One of the key turning points in the Pacific Theater of World War II was the Battle of Midway, fought from June 4 to June 7, 1942. The battle, which took place six months after the attack on Pearl Harbor, was a decisive victory for the United States Navy over the Imperial Japanese Navy. The American victory at Midway halted the Japanese advance in the Pacific and turned the tide of the war in favor of the Allies, marking the beginning of the end for Japanese expansionism.

D-Day and the Normandy Invasion

In the European Theater of World War II, one of the most significant turning points was the Allied invasion of Normandy, also known as D-Day, on June 6, 1944. The largest amphibious assault in history, D-Day saw Allied forces, led by American, British, and Canadian troops, landing on the beaches of Normandy in northern France to liberate Western Europe from Nazi occupation. The successful invasion of Normandy opened a second front against Nazi Germany and paved the way for the eventual defeat of Hitler's Third Reich.

Battle of Stalingrad

In the Eastern Front of World War II, one of the most pivotal battles was the Battle of Stalingrad, fought from August 23, 1942, to February 2, 1943. The battle, which pitted German forces against Soviet defenders in the city of Stalingrad (now Volgograd) in southern Russia, was one of the bloodiest and most brutal battles of the war. The Soviet victory at Stalingrad marked a turning point in the war on the Eastern Front and dealt a severe blow to the German war machine, weakening Hitler's grip on Eastern Europe and setting the stage for the Soviet advance towards Berlin.

Conclusion

America's entry into World War II marked a turning point in the conflict and had profound implications for the outcome of the war and the course of world history. The attack on Pearl Harbor galvanized the American people and propelled the United States into a total war effort to defeat the Axis powers. The home front mobilization of industry and the sacrifices made by millions of Americans on the home front played a crucial role in supporting the Allied war effort and securing victory in World War II. Key battles and turning points in the war, such as the Battle of Midway, D-Day, and the Battle of Stalingrad, helped to turn the tide of the war in favor of the Allies and ultimately led to the defeat of Nazi Germany, Imperial Japan, and Fascist Italy.

Chapter 15: The Cold War and Beyond

The Cold War was a period of geopolitical tension and ideological rivalry between the United States and the Soviet Union that lasted from the end of World War II in 1945 until the collapse of the Soviet Union in 1991. This chapter will delve into the origins of the Cold War and America's role in the conflict, the civil rights movement and the fight for equality, and America's position in the post-Cold War era and its role in the world today.

Origins of the Cold War and America's Role

The Yalta and Potsdam Conferences

The seeds of the Cold War were sown during World War II, as tensions between the United States and the Soviet Union began to emerge over issues such as postwar reconstruction, territorial boundaries, and the future of Eastern Europe. The Yalta Conference in February 1945 and the Potsdam Conference in July-August 1945, where the leaders of the Allied powers met to discuss the postwar order, highlighted the growing distrust and suspicion between the United States and the Soviet Union. Despite their wartime alliance against Nazi Germany, the United States and the Soviet Union held fundamentally different visions for the postwar world, leading to increasing tensions and rivalries.

The Division of Europe

The division of Europe into Western and Eastern blocs emerged as a central feature of the Cold War, as the United States and its Western allies sought to contain the spread of communism and Soviet influence, while the Soviet Union sought to expand its sphere of influence and establish communist governments in Eastern Europe. The Truman Doctrine, announced by President Harry Truman in 1947, pledged American support for nations threatened by communist expansionism, while the Marshall Plan, initiated in 1948, provided economic aid to Western European countries to help rebuild their war-torn economies and resist communist influence.

The Arms Race and Nuclear Proliferation

The Cold War also witnessed a massive arms race between the United States and the Soviet Union, as both superpowers sought to build up their military arsenals and stockpiles of nuclear weapons in a bid to deter each other from launching a nuclear attack. The development of nuclear weapons and the threat of mutually assured destruction (MAD) created a precarious balance of power between the two superpowers, as both sides sought to avoid direct confrontation while engaging in a dangerous game of brinkmanship and proxy conflicts.

The Civil Rights Movement and the Fight for Equality

Segregation and Discrimination

While the United States was engaged in the Cold War abroad, it also faced significant challenges at home, particularly in the area of civil rights and racial equality. Despite the end of slavery and the passage of constitutional amendments guaranteeing equal rights and protections for all citizens, African Americans continued to face widespread segregation, discrimination, and disenfranchisement in many parts of the country. Jim Crow laws enforced racial segregation and discrimination in public facilities, schools, and accommodations, while acts of violence and terrorism, such as lynching and the Ku Klux Klan, targeted African Americans who dared to challenge the status quo.

The Civil Rights Movement

The civil rights movement of the 1950s and 1960s emerged as a grassroots movement to challenge racial segregation and discrimination and secure equal rights and opportunities for African Americans. Led by figures such as Martin Luther King Jr., Rosa Parks, and Malcolm X, the civil rights movement employed nonviolent protest tactics such as sit-ins, boycotts, and marches to bring attention to the injustices of segregation and demand change. Landmark events such as the Montgomery Bus Boycott, the March on Washington, and the Selma to Montgomery marches galvanized public support for the civil rights cause and led to legislative victories such as the Civil Rights Act of 1964 and the Voting Rights Act of 1965.

Legacy of the Civil Rights Movement

The civil rights movement had a profound and lasting impact on American society and culture, as it challenged entrenched notions of white supremacy and segregation and paved the way for greater equality and justice for all Americans. The movement not only secured legal and political rights for African Americans but also inspired other marginalized groups to demand their rights and fight for social justice, leading to the emergence of movements for women's rights, LGBTQ+ rights, and the rights of other minority groups.

America in the Post-Cold War Era and Its Role in the World Today

Collapse of the Soviet Union

The Cold War came to an end in 1991 with the collapse of the Soviet Union and the dissolution of the Eastern bloc. The end of the Cold War ushered in a new era of geopolitical realignment and uncertainty, as the United States emerged as the world's sole superpower and the dominant force in global affairs. The collapse of the Soviet Union marked the triumph of capitalism and democracy over communism and authoritarianism, but it also created new challenges and opportunities for the United States as it sought to navigate a rapidly changing world order.

Globalization and Technological Advancements

The post-Cold War era has been characterized by rapid globalization and technological advancements that have transformed the way people live, work, and communicate. The rise of the internet and digital technology has facilitated the global exchange of information, ideas, and commerce, while advances in transportation and communication have made the world more interconnected and interdependent than ever before. These developments have created new opportunities for economic growth and prosperity but have also brought about new challenges and vulnerabilities, such as cyber threats, economic inequality, and environmental degradation.

America's Role in the World Today

In the post-Cold War era, the United States continues to play a leading role in global affairs, as it seeks to promote democracy, human rights, and free-market capitalism around the world. However, America's role in the world today is increasingly complex and contested, as it grapples with emerging threats and challenges such as terrorism, nuclear proliferation, climate change, and geopolitical competition from rising powers such as China and Russia. The United States faces pressing domestic challenges as well, including political polarization, economic inequality, and social unrest, which threaten to undermine its global leadership and influence.

Conclusion

The Cold War and its aftermath have had a profound and lasting impact on American society, politics, and culture. The origins of the Cold War can be traced back to the tensions and rivalries that emerged in the aftermath of World War II, as the United States and the Soviet Union vied for dominance on the world stage. The civil rights movement of the 1950s and 1960s challenged the injustices of segregation and discrimination and laid the groundwork for greater equality and justice for all Americans. In the post-Cold War era, the United States continues to grapple with new challenges and opportunities as it seeks to maintain its position as a global superpower and navigate a rapidly changing world order.

Don't miss out!

Visit the website below and you can sign up to receive emails whenever Michael Johnson publishes a new book. There's no charge and no obligation.

https://books2read.com/r/B-A-OREFB-MNVZC

About the Author

Michael Johnson is a distinguished historian specializing in American history. With a degree in History from Harvard University, Johnson's work delves into pivotal moments, figures, and themes shaping the United States. He has authored numerous acclaimed books, offering insightful perspectives and engaging narratives. Johnson's commitment to meticulous scholarship and compelling storytelling has earned him widespread acclaim in the field. Passionate about sharing his expertise, he frequently engages in lectures and public events to foster a deeper appreciation for America's past.

9 798224 670772